BOOK ANALYSIS

By Claire Parker

The Blind Assassin

BY MARGARET ATWOOD

Bright
≡Summaries.com

MARGARET ATWOOD

CANADIAN NOVELIST, POET AND ESSAYIST

- **Born in Ottawa in 1939.**
- **Notable works:**
  - *The Handmaid's Tale* (1985), novel
  - *Alias Grace* (1996), novel
  - *Oryx and Crake* (2003), novel

Margaret Atwood is Canada's most influential contemporary writer. She studied English Literature at the University of Toronto and later at Harvard, and first received public acclaim as a poet in the 1960s with her collections *Double Persephone* (1961) and *The Circle Game* (1966). She has since written over 40 works including novels, short stories and critical essays which have been published around the world, though she is perhaps most famous for her 1985 dystopian novel *The Handmaid's Tale*. Her impressive range of work spans science fiction, myth, life writing and historical fiction, but is largely united by themes of abuse of power and female experience: "My women suffer because most of the women I speak to seem to have suffered", she has said (Klemesrud, 1982). Atwood's later work also explores the process of writing, and as an English lecturer she delivered a series of lectures in 2000 entitled *Negotiating with the Dead: A Writer on Writing*. She currently lives in Toronto.

THE BLIND ASSASSIN

A MULTI-TIERED NOVEL

- **Genre:** novel
- **Reference edition:** Atwood, M. (2009) *The Blind Assassin*. London: Virago Press.
- **1st edition:** 2000
- **Themes:** betrayal, sacrifice, power, vengeance, mystery, storytelling

"Ten days after the war ended, my sister Laura drove a car off a bridge" (p. 3). In this, *The Blind Assassin*'s very first sentence, we are presented with a mystery which shapes the entire book. Discovering the truth of why Laura Chase killed herself is at the heart of Atwood's complex multi-tiered novel, which is narrated, albeit unreliably, by Laura's sister Iris in the form of a fragmentary memoir which alternates between past and present. Atwood's book has a highly unconventional structure, spanning several genres and including a novel-within-a-novel attributed to Laura, also called *The Blind Assassin*. Set in 20th-century Canada, Atwood's novel tells the story of Iris and Laura's entwined lives from childhood to adulthood, and through their involvement with two diametrically opposed male characters. *The Blind Assassin* was awarded the 2000 Booker Prize and remains one of Atwood's better-known novels.

SUMMARY

STORIES WITHIN STORIES

Iris Chase, daughter of the once-successful businessman Norval Chase, is old, frail, and spends her time listening to local weather reports or being visited by doctors. Writing in her old age in Ontario, she describes herself as "a local fixture, a vacant lot where some important building used to stand" (p. 54). However, where Iris is now isolated, her younger sister Laura is far from being forgotten, achieving much posthumous acclaim as a novelist following her tragic suicide as a young woman. In her memoir, Iris recalls the events that led up to the day her sister drove off a bridge, but the memoir's structure is not conventional or chronological, and the truth not easily revealed. Instead, the first-person narration is interwoven with newspaper clippings and extracts from Laura's novel, also called *The Blind Assassin*, which was published by Iris on behalf of her dead sister. The extracts of this novel tell the story of a clandestine affair between a man and a woman (whom the reader assumes to be Laura) who remain nameless, who construct fantastical science-fiction stories together as they conduct their relationship. One of these stories, set in the city of Sakeil-Norn on the planet Zycron, tells how children blinded by the intricate forced labour of making beautiful carpets were often later hired as assassins (hence the novel's name), so heightened had their other senses become.

AVILION

Iris remembers how she and her younger sister Laura were raised on an estate called Avilion, a "merchant's palace" (p. 72) whose name was taken from a poem by Tennyson, and which had been bought with the profits from their grandfather's successful button-manufacturing business. When Iris and Laura are very young, their mother dies following a traumatic miscarriage in the family kitchen, and in her final moments Iris's mother makes her promise to look after her younger sister because Laura is vulnerable and, as their maid Reenie says, "not the same as other people" (p. 110). Iris envies Laura's difference while simultaneously feeling very protective of her little sister.

The two girls do not go to school, and are visited instead by private tutors, one of whom is the "hair-puller" (p. 197) and "ear-twister" (*ibid.*) Mr Erskine. Laura refuses to learn under him and dislikes writing, instead preferring to make curious drawings by covering black and white photos in bright, expressionistic colours which, she thinks, show the true nature of a thing or person. Eventually, Laura gets Mr Erskine dismissed by claiming he put his hands up her blouse. Iris writes that what she learned from him was "half-concealed insolence and silent resistance" (p. 203).

THE PICNIC

At their annual picnic, the Chase family receive Mr Richard Griffen, a rival businessman who had previously publicly attacked the girls' father Norval for being "too soft on the unemployed" (p. 213). Also attending is a young, dark-haired man called Alex Thomas. Alex is an orphan raised by a Presbyterian minister who loathes the rich and powerful business elite, and Laura is completely captivated by him. At the picnic, a photo is taken for the local press of Iris and Laura sat either side of Alex "like bookends" (p. 234). Soon after, the authorities start looking for Alex, accusing him of being a spy and of setting fire to Norval Chase's button factory. Iris discovers that Laura has hidden Alex in the attic, and together, the two sisters bring him scraps of food as well as paper and a pencil at his request. Once, when Iris goes to see Alex alone, he kisses her, and she wonders if he has done the same to Laura. When hiding Alex becomes too risky, he flees for Spain, leaving behind only a list of made-up words in the attic – words the reader recognises from the science-fiction stories of 'Laura's novel' *The Blind Assassin*. After Alex's escape, Laura gives Iris a copy of the photo of the three of them from the picnic which she has cut herself out of, except for her hand. "That's what you want to remember" (p. 269), she tells her sister, which Iris interprets as "the closest she ever came [...] to a confession of love for Alex Thomas" (*ibid.*). Laura explains she also made a copy of the photo for herself, but mirrored; this time, Iris has been cut out, leaving only Laura and Alex.

A CONVENIENT ARRANGEMENT

The Great Depression takes its toll on the Chase business, and Norval arranges a marriage between Richard Griffen and the 18-year-old Iris in exchange for his help to keep the business afloat. Laura begs her sister not to enter a loveless marriage, but Iris maintains that it is the sensible thing to do, agreeing "to open my legs and shut my mouth" (p. 407). But her sacrifice is in vain: Norval announces the permanent closure of his factories and dies during Iris's honeymoon, she suspects as a result of his heavy drinking. Following Norval's death, Richard and his controlling sister Winifred decide that, as a minor aged 14, Laura should come and live with them. There, both Laura and Iris see Alex Thomas walking on the street on separate occasions – when Laura mentions this, Iris tells her coldly that if she has a crush on him she should try to get over it. Meanwhile, in 'Laura's novel' *The Blind Assassin*, the two lovers continue their affair, and the reader assumes its protagonists are Laura and Alex.

One day, Winifred tells Iris that Laura has "snapped" (p. 523) and that, delusional and convinced she is pregnant, she has been placed into the care of an institution called Bella Vista, which Iris is strictly forbidden to visit. Meanwhile, Iris gives birth to a daughter who is born with a thick head of dark hair. The fact that Richard and Iris are both fair-haired suggests that it is Alex Thomas, not her husband, who is the father. Meanwhile, in the novel-within-a-novel, the male protagonist is on the run and, after a period of worry and torment, the woman receives a telegram confirming that her lover has died in the war.

REVELATIONS

Iris finally meets up with Laura after their former housekeeper Reenie helps her escape from Bella Vista. Far from delusional and confused, Laura seems completely sane, contrary to what Iris's husband and sister-in-law have told her. Laura tells her sister she had genuinely fallen pregnant, and that she had been forcibly sent to Bella Vista to have an abortion. Iris assumes Alex was the father of her unborn child and, partly out of anger, reveals that she herself had been Alex's lover, and that she had received a telegram informing her of his death. At this, Laura grabs Iris's car keys and disappears; only later does Iris find out that Laura had driven the car off of a bridge, dying instantly.

When Iris finds one of Laura's childhood exercise books and reads the words Laura had written for her, she discovers the truth – the real father of Laura's developing baby was not Alex Thomas but Richard Griffen. It transpires that the latter had been sexually abusing Laura, threatening to turn Alex Thomas in to the authorities unless she complied. As a final plot twist, Iris reveals to the reader that she, not Laura, is the author of *The Blind Assassin*, and that Laura may never have had an affair with Alex at all. Iris had known that by sacrificing her authorship of the book and granting Laura posthumous acclaim, people might realise that it was Richard's behaviour which drove her to suicide. This indeed happens: his political career ruined, Richard kills himself, and Iris remains alone. But through her memoir, she memorialises herself, dedicating her memoir to her granddaughter Sabrina, who is "the last of us" (p. 231) and whom she hopes will one day know the truth it contains.

CHARACTER STUDY

IRIS CHASE

Iris is the first-person narrator of *The Blind Assassin*, as well as the protagonist of the novel-within-a-novel of the same name. In the present, she describes herself as "an urn in daylight" (p. 54), a frail figure who is frequently "too tired to do much more than lie on the sofa" (p. 547). But Iris is also characterised as a somewhat passive figure in her youth; when Laura colours in photos of her, for example, they are always blue because, Laura explains, Iris is "asleep" (p. 238). This passivity leads to a sense of loss of self on her honeymoon, following her agreement to marry Richard to save the (ultimately doomed) family business: "each time I looked in the mirror a little bit of me had been coloured in" (p. 370). "I was sand, I was snow – written on, rewritten, smoothed over" (p. 394), she admits.

However, despite this passivity, Iris is partly to blame for Laura's suicide, and as such Iris could be said to be the novel's true 'blind assassin'. Iris's relationship with Laura is characterised by both love and spite, and this is infinitely complicated by the arrival of Alex Thomas, who charms both sisters. Though Iris has solemnly promised her parents to look after her younger sister, she worries that Laura is having an affair with Alex. Torn between her love for Laura and her love for Alex, Iris turns a blind eye to Winifred and Richard's harsh treatment of her sister when she is put into their care. It is only later that she discovers the full extent of Richard's abuse towards her sister. Iris's last act of atonement ("Better late than never", she thinks, p. 445) is to catapult Laura into posthumous fame and thereby incriminate Richard, though in so doing she condemns herself to a life of isolation and loneliness.

LAURA CHASE

Laura is Iris's younger sister; the news of her tragic death opens the novel, and the circumstances which led up to it drive the plot forward, culminating in a great dénouement. However, Laura herself remains a largely enigmatic figure, not least because, although we assume that she is the protagonist of the novel-within-a-novel, it is revealed to be the story of her sister's affair, not hers. Far from being a gifted novelist, then, the reader eventually learns that "Laura wrote like an angel. In other words, not very much" (p. 608).

From her early childhood, Laura is characterised as both vulnerable and defiant. For example, she gets her tutor Mr Erskine dismissed by accusing him of molesting her, using her victimhood as a form of power. She is deeply pious as a child, and has a great sense of social responsibility, but her idea of sacrifice is sometimes misplaced. For example, after the death of her mother, she tries to make a bargain with God whereby he will bring her mother back if she jumps into a deep river (from which Iris has to save her). Laura interprets the world around her in a powerful yet literal way; when Reenie tells her to be "thankful for small mercies" (p. 44), Laura replies "Why should we be? Why are they so small?" (*ibid.*), and after being told that "God is everywhere" (p. 168), Laura begins to worry about God's exact location, asking: "Is he under the bed?" (*ibid.*). It is precisely this way of thinking which makes Laura different but also vulnerable, and although Iris reacts to her vulnerability with a desire to protect her, she reacts to her difference with envy. Laura is prepared to sacrifice her body to prevent Richard from betraying Alex Thomas's whereabouts, and she endures Richard's rape and a forced abortion – but the implied betrayal through her sister Iris's affair with Alex, as well as the latter's death, is what ultimately drives her to suicide.

The ways in which Laura and Iris's characters are mirrored by Atwood is captured in the motif of the photograph taken at the Labour Day picnic, with Iris and Laura either side of Alex Thomas. Each girl keeps a copy of the photo with the other one cut out, so the copies of the photographs perfectly mirror each other. This mirroring is echoed later on when the two women become pregnant, Laura by Iris's husband and Iris by Alex Thomas, whom she assumes to also be Laura's lover. Both sisters make sacrifices to save men – Iris, by marrying Richard to save her father's business, and Laura by allowing Richard's abuse of her in order to save Alex Thomas. Laura and Iris are also mirror images of each other in 'Laura's novel', and for much of the book the reader is unaware which sister is the novel-within-a-novel's true protagonist. The complexity of Laura and Iris's relationship, with its subtle betrayals and acts of love, is what gives Atwood's novel its psychological depth, and is characteristic of her work, which foregrounds relationships between women within male-dominated power structures.

ALEX THOMAS

Alex Thomas is a political radical and revolutionary whom Iris and Laura hide in their attic after he is accused of being a spy. He captivates both Chase sisters, though arguably uses them both, and at times Alex's behaviour is morally questionable at best. His initial kiss, though it leads to a passionate affair with Iris, is closer to sexual assault than a romantic gesture. And even while the two conduct their affair, Alex can be argumentative, insulting and even violent towards his lover. He is also repulsed by the rich and powerful elite, and tries unsuccessfully to persuade Iris to leave her industrialist husband. Alex is a convincing storyteller, not only of the other-worldly tales he tells within the novel-within-a-novel, but also in convincing the sisters that he is innocent of the crimes he is accused of (something which remains unresolved throughout the book). After he flees, Laura protects Alex through her sexual self-sacrifice to Richard, and from then on he remains a taboo topic of conversation between Iris and Laura. Alex's ultimate death in the Second World War, and the naming of Iris, not Laura, as his next of kin, become pivotal factors in Laura's decision to take her own life.

REENIE

Reenie is a long-standing employee of the Chase family, working at Avilion as a maid and nanny. Though she is presented as a gossiping and meddling figure ("She was the town interpreter, mine and Laura's", p. 37), she is also one of the novel's most sympathetic characters. After the death of Iris and Laura's mother, Reenie takes on a maternal role at Avilion; she was "always there" (p. 5) and "felt that who we were ought to be enough for anybody" (p. 285), and Iris in her adulthood has often wished she would come back and "take care of her" (p. 450). Reenie helps Laura escape from the nightmarish Bella Vista by

pretending to be her lawyer, and also gives her a
key (which she has kept despite being dismissed
by the villainous Richard) so Laura can revisit her
family home. Reenie refuses to kiss Iris the last
time she sees her, recognising Iris' silent betrayal
of her sister. Her help and maternal presence is
recalled through the character of her daughter
Myra, who looks after Iris in her old age and
prevents her from being completely isolated and
alone.

RICHARD GRIFFEN

Richard Griffen is a greedy and ambitious industrialist who is perhaps the most one-dimensional
character in *The Blind Assassin*. A rather clichéd
villainous figure, Richard is a Nazi sympathiser
who psychologically controls his wife (whom he
has never loved and makes sexually submissive)
and impregnates his sister-in-law by raping her.
He enjoys the power he has over both Chase
sisters, "preferr[ing] conquest to cooperation, in
any area of life" (p. 454), and does not keep his
business promises to their father Norval Chase,
which may have contributed to the latter's
suicide. Iris recognises that Richard's character

lacks depth in her memoirs: "I've failed to convey Richard, in any rounded sense" (p. 585). For, to her, "he's blurred, like some wet, discarded newspaper" (*ibid.*) who occupies a very small part of her inner life, despite seeming to control it. Richard eventually experiences his downfall because of Iris's decision to publish her novel under Laura's name, reopening the inquest into her death. He is found dead, having committed suicide, on one of his sailing boats.

ANALYSIS

THE SEARCH FOR TRUTH

"The living bird is not its labelled bones", writes Iris (p. 484). A conventional murder mystery story starts with a death and slowly unravels the truth. *The Blind Assassin* follows this pattern to some extent, but is complicated by a narrator who is only too conscious of her own unreliability. Writing in her eighties, Iris is attempting to piece together a narrative of the events that took place over 70 years ago (and, in some cases, in the even more distant past), even though she has previously taken an active role in concealing the truth of these events. She therefore does not rely on her own narrative voice alone, but also draws on a wide variety of other sources, from history books to newspaper articles to Reenie's anecdotes. The resulting form of her memoir is a kind of collage, a collection of fragments which the reader must attempt to piece together like clues. But even this kind of scrapbooking of events does not bring Iris closer to the truth, for "the only way you can write the truth is to assume what you write will never be read" (p. 345). Besides, even the newspaper cuttings from the *Toronto Star*, which the reader might initially assume to present the facts, are shown to be misinformed at various points.

Iris also questions her own memories and interpretations of past events. For example, when she recalls how Alex started kissing her when she visited him alone in the attic, she says: "I hadn't expected this. Had I expected this? Was it so sudden, or were there preliminaries: a touch, a gaze? Did I do anything to provoke him? Nothing I can recall, but is what I remember the same thing as what actually happened?" (p. 226). However, this uncertainty also gives Iris an awareness of the nebulous nature of 'the truth': "Two and two doesn't necessarily get you the truth. Two and two equals a voice outside the window. Two and two equals the wind" (p. 484).

Despite this, Iris clearly longs to capture the essence of 'the truth' in her memoir to her granddaughter, which can be contrasted with Alex Thomas' desire to create fiction in the fantastical and deliberately exaggerated stories he tells to his lover during their affair. However, despite their other-worldliness, the stories often shed more light on the characters' predicaments than Iris's memories of the real events; for example, the story of the blind assassin who must either betray the girl he falls in love with or run away with her forever recalls the way the novel's characters are often torn between love and responsibility. Ultimately, *The Blind Assassin* is a musing on the process of remembering, how quickly a lie can become the truth (or vice versa) and how a misremembrance can change the course of history.

THE POWER OF THE WRITTEN WORD

In 'Laura's novel', when the male protagonist offers to change the story for his lover, to "rewrite history" for her (p. 37) the lover replies, "You can't. The word has gone forth" (p. 38). In Atwood's novel, the written word has a power greater than any human character, living or dead (after all, it is the appearance of words alone that catapult Laura to posthumous fame); though we are told that Laura would "make her mark"

(p. 374), it is the physical, written marks on the page that ultimately hold power. Although Laura takes words at face value as a child, taking their literal meanings to extremes, it is Iris who understands the power of storytelling, committing pen to paper. Iris is hyper-conscious of this, and as she writes her memoirs, she muses: "On this page [...] I will cause the war to end – I alone, with a stroke of my black plastic pen" (p. 93). This is deeply ironic – although Iris is only referring to the end of the First World War, it is precisely with her black plastic pen that she wages an altogether different war – the one which will avenge Laura's death.

It is the discovery or indeed the disappearance of words on a page that drives the plot forward in many instances in Atwood's novel. Richard intercepts and destroys telegrams that Laura has tried to send to Iris, leaving the latter unaware of her sister's suffering; the words that Alex Thomas leaves in the attic at Avilion are proof to the reader, if they were in any doubt, of Alex's identity as the storyteller protagonist in the novel-within-a-novel; and when her lover has fled, the female protagonist of 'Laura's novel' searches desperately through book and magazine shops looking for the next instalment of Alex's science fiction story, since its publication would prove her lover's survival. The fact that the stories are deeply intertwined with the lovers' sexual encounters adds to this sense of the 'physicality' of writing. And, in the novel's dramatic climax, Iris discovers the truth about Richard's assault of Laura through notebooks that she has left her. In addition, the multi-tiered nature of Atwood's novel – the stories within stories within stories – makes the reader question which forms of writing we trust the most.

LEGACY

Questions surrounding 'legacy' in *The Blind Assassin* get right to the heart of the instances of betrayal and sacrifice throughout the book. At the start of the novel, Iris is all but forgotten. She stands in a university giving out the 'Laura Chase Memorial Prize Creative Writing' while the proud students do not so much as look at her. The deep irony, of course, is that Iris is the true author of the novel that brought Laura so much posthumous success. This, then, is why Iris is so protective over the rights and opportunities surrounding Laura's book, writing "terse replies" which she describes as "venomous doodling" (p. 350) to interested inquirers. However, at this point it is not Laura she is protecting but herself. Indeed, we get the impression that, though Iris made this sacrifice for Laura, she resents not having her own memorial, hence the memoir that we are reading: "Why is it we want to badly to memorialise ourselves? Even while we're still alive. We wish to exert our existence, like dogs peeing on fire hydrants" (p. 118). It is also worth noting that, though the publication of *The Blind Assassin* under Laura's name does bring justice for Laura and incriminates Richard, it also has disastrous unintended consequences. When the novel is published, one of its readers is Aimee, Iris's daughter with Alex Thomas. Aimee concludes from the book that Laura is her real mother, and therefore that both of her parents are dead. She is psychologically damaged by this false revelation and turns to drugs, which leads to a fatal fall. The act of protecting her sister's legacy therefore leads to the death of Iris's own daughter. It is thus that, in Atwood's novel, a selfless act can also be a selfish one, and an act of sacrifice can also be an act of betrayal.

BLINDNESS

The title of Atwood's novel has both a literal and a metaphorical meaning. Alex's science-fiction stories, related in the novel-within-a-novel, tell of a trained killer who lost his sight as a child – a literal 'blind assassin'. However, in the broader context of Atwood's novel, the title takes on a metaphorical significance related to culpability surrounding Laura's death, through which Atwood explores the themes of wilful or unknowing blindness to the consequences of one's actions. Even though Laura made the decision to take her own life, she was arguably driven to it by the actions of others: by closing her eyes to Richard's mistreatment of Laura, Iris commits an act of betrayal. As well as this, she fails to heed the consequences of revealing Alex's death, and her own affair with him, to Laura in her already delicate state. Both of these betrayals contribute to Laura's decision to commit suicide. But ironically, by trying to make amends to her sister by catapulting her to posthumous fame and launching an inquest into her death, Iris indirectly causes the death of her own daughter: the latter reaches false conclusions about her own family history, propelling her into a downward spiral that eventually claims her life. In this way, Iris could be seen as the true blind assassin. It is through the theme of blindness that Atwood is able to explore complex issues of guilt and responsibility; almost every character commits acts of betrayal, however small, against those they love, but are blind to their consequences.

FURTHER REFLECTION

SOME QUESTIONS TO THINK ABOUT...

- Who are the various 'blind assassins' in Atwood's novel who uncomprehendingly bring about others' demise? Is there any character who does not commit an act of betrayal, however small?
- Iris acknowledges that "the living bird is not its labelled bones" (p. 484). In the light of this remark, in what ways is Iris an unreliable narrator, either consciously or unconsciously?
- Compare the influences that Reenie and Winifred Griffen respectively have on Iris. In what ways could both be said to act as maternal figures?
- What role do newspaper clippings play in *The Blind Assassin*? To what extent are they objective sources of information?
- How do the reader's sympathies towards Iris change as she describes different stages of her life?

- Sometimes the story leaps forward in time with pieces of crucial information, the significance of which we only understand later on. In what ways does this heighten suspense in the novel?
- "For whom am I writing this? For myself? I think not" (p. 53). Whose legacy does Iris protect most – her sister's or her own?
- In what ways do the science fiction stories created by the unnamed lovers in Laura's novel mirror the real characters? What similarities are there between the planet Zygron and the Canada that Iris describes throughout her life?
- Have you read any other works by Margaret Atwood? If so, how do the themes in this novel compare or differ?

We want to hear from you!
Leave a comment on your online library
and share your favourite books on social media!

FURTHER READING

REFERENCE EDITION

- Atwood, M. (2009) *The Blind Assassin*. London: Virago Press.

ADDITIONAL SOURCES

- Howells, C. A. ed. (2007) *The Cambridge Companion to Margaret Atwood*. Cambridge: Cambridge University Press.

- Klemesrud, J. (1982) 'High Priestess of Angst'. *The New York Times*. [Online]. [Accessed 31 January 2019]. Available from: <http://movies2.nytimes.com/books/00/09/03/specials/atwood-angst.html>

MORE FROM BRIGHTSUMMARIES.COM

- Reading guide – *The Handmaid's Tale* by Margaret Atwood.

www.brightsummaries.com

Ebook EAN: 9782808017329

Paperback EAN: 9782808017336

Legal Deposit: D/2019/12603/33

Cover: © Primento

Digital conception by Primento, the digital partner of
publishers.

Printed in Great Britain
by Amazon

22304456R00031